Life Will Always Throw You Curve Balls. It's Your Job To Swing The Bat.
Motivational Quote Lined Notebook
Motivational Journals for Women
Paperback ISBN: 978-1-989733-22-6
Published by Dunhill Clare Publishing 2020
All Rights Reserved. Cover Design by Sharon Purtill

www.ingramcontent.com/pod-product-compliance
Lightning Source LLC
Chambersburg PA
CBHW071249070526
44583CB00017B/2389